THE

VOICE

IN THE

VOLKSWAGEN

THE *For tay~*

VOICE

IN THE

VOLKSWAGEN

by
Marjorie Johana Moon Goldberg-Garrison

Gammy.

Drawings by
Laddy Barnett and *Kristin Konvolinka*

©2014 Johana Goldberg-Garrison
ISBN 13: 978-1-58790-287-1
ISBN 10: 1-58790-287-7
Library of Congress Control Number: 2014947332

Drawings by: Laddy Barnett
                    Kristin Konvolinka

Crafted in the U.S.A
Regent Press
www.regentpress.net

The Voice in the Volkswagen

PHASES

Phase One

Not So Cozy Nest

THE VOICE IN THE VOLKSWAGEN

Not So Cozy Next

Mystical Daydream

    I am a child, laying in a meadow with flowers and grass and bees humming around me. The sun is shining but not hot. A gentle breeze mingles me with the flowers and the grass and the bees and the humming. I remember having long, slender arms, reaching up, and a child's innocent body. Looking up, I knew all was glorious!

He Said a Prayer and Cried

My Dad was loving, playful and kind. He sang, recited poetry – *Dangerous Dan McGrew* – taught me to catch a ball, ride a bike, hammer a nail and saw a board. Every Thanksgiving he said a prayer, cried and wiped his nose. I loved those tears.

My Religious Guidance

Before my memory was formed, Mother taught me the Lord's Prayer. It is as though I had known it all my life! We never **said** the Lord's Prayer. I just knew I knew it. That Thanksgiving prayer and knowing the Lord's Prayer – but not understanding what it meant - was my entire religious background. We did sing Christmas Carols; I never understood their meaning. They were beautiful and fun to sing.

When I married Fred, which I will get into later, my Grandmother Moon, upon learning I was marrying a Jewish man, said, "How can you give up your Jesus?" Since I knew nothing about the Jewish people and the Old Testament and Christ, I didn't know what she was talking about. I remember her saying that. Years later, I tried to read Grandma's Bible – it didn't make any sense to me.

My Sister

I was 18 months older than Cathie. We shared our young years and were important to one another. We were pals and playmates.

Cathie and I clung together in those times when Mom and Dad were drinking and quarreling.

Mother

During the day, Mom tended to business: caring for the home, washing clothes, ironing and paying the bills. She did it all without complaint. Cathie and I asked our Mother about sex – what it was all about and how it worked. She seemed shaken. She didn't answer our questions but said, "I thought if you didn't know anything about it, you wouldn't be interested." Ha!

At times, Mom showed us her albums and told us about her high school days and her boyfriends. She'd bring out her diamond rings and tell us the history of each one. You'll meet one of these diamonds a little later. She became fun and animated during these moments. When I say "us", that is always Cathie and me.

Wrong Interpretation

Mother adored Cathie. I held Mother hostage to my suspicion that I was not loved by my mother as she loved Cathie. The suspicion melded into anger and defiance, which as you will see, got me into a lot of trouble. I adopted a sullen blaming attitude toward my Mother, concluding, "You love Cathie more than me."

Sister Marilyn said, "I remember you standing in the hall, resting your head on your arm, and crying." If you saw pictures of me as a child you would see one glum kid.

In those days, no one knew anything about psychology or counseling or how to talk to an estranged child. Dad, sensing I needed support, leaned in my direction. I always believed I "had" Daddy "on my side".

The Cedar Chest

One day, as Cathie and I were rummaging through Mother's Cedar Chest in the garage, we discovered our Mother had been married before she wed our Father. We were shocked. We took our discovery to our Mother. She confessed. His name was Clarence. She said, "He was too nice. I was bored."

Daddy, a Raconteur

Mom wasn't bored with my Dad! Mom was fascinated with my fun loving, song singing, cigarette smoking, liquor-drinking Dad. Moma reminisced, "When he came out of the shower, his red hair was in ringlets." Every night, before he came home from work, she'd say, "Your Dad's on his way home - have to powder my nose."

Mom and Dad

Daddy taught Mom how to smoke, drink and gamble. Apparently, she was willing. They both prized the reckless action of gambling, traveling to Reno, Las Vegas, Santa Anita and Hollywood Park. When Mom saw Bing Crosby there, she asked, "Hi Bing. Got a tip?" Bing's tip, "Keep your money in your pocket."

From Mother to Monster

Daddy was outgoing, fun and joyful; Mother was stoic, quiet, thoughtful, and clever UNTIL she had a drink. While Dad with his easy going, swaying with the breeze ways, tolerated smoking and liquor, they tossed Mother like a tempest. Every night Daddy brought home a bottle of whiskey. Liquor had a terrible effect on Mother. She became angry, hostile and argumentative. One whiff and her countenance changed from my Mother into a monster. Her eyes branded blistering fury as her face twisted into revulsion. No wonder the film Dr. Jekyll and Mr. Hyde frightened me so!!

"I Lost. We Have to Leave."

On their honeymoon, he went downstairs to gamble, lost all of their money, came to their room and said, "We have to leave." Apparently, in addition to the honeymoon letdown, he had a fling with someone which action broke her heart. From that time on, the happy-go-lucky ways of my Father, which had so charmed her, distorted to become the target for her deep Scottish angst, punctuated by the awful effect liquor had on her emotions. She loved and adored him AND she was angry with him as long as I can remember.

"Rot in Hell"

She routinely brought that up in her drunken tirade against him. Under the influence, they fought with words in passionate, damaging ways. The thing I remember the most is Mother saying, "I hope you rot in Hell." They were disgusting and frightening.

Two little girls, clinging together, watched in fear and horror as their parents argued, fought and insulted one another in a nightly ritual.

The Good Guy

Dad, escaping Hell, mostly defended himself and tried to quiet her. He portrayed himself as the "good guy" even though it was he who introduced her to smoking, drinking and gambling. Dad was not overtly hostile - he **was** the one who brought the liquor home!!! There were times when he was going to the store to get another bottle, we begged him, "No, no, Daddy. Don't go." He always went. Somehow, he got something out of the terrible scene.

The next day, after the wild, drunken arena, Moma acted as though nothing had happened, that she had not said those terrible words or behaved in that horrible way. And that night, it happened all over again!

We Both Studied Psychology!

Mother and Dad as models were strange ones. While Daddy was happy and fun, Mom was quiet and solidly stable. Other than Mother's epitaph regarding Daddy's afterlife and their drunken arguments, their language was polite, courteous and helpful. Mother possessed an admirable vocabulary. Cathie agrees that Mother's hidden, aching emotions were released by alcohol, which was probably a psychologically medicating remedy for her. It is no wonder that Cathie and I ardently pursued studies to understand psychology and its connected behaviors.

So Long, Letty

Once in a while, Mom joined Dad in a happy mood and they sang together. Daddy had a beautiful Irish tenor voice; Mother had an alto voice. They had a song they sang together. I've never heard it anywhere else. It was, So Long Letty, Good Bye. They'd sit, shoulder to shoulder, singing, *I'll miss you, So Long, Letty, Good Bye*. A plaintive plea. I have a sheet music of the song framed and hanging in my bath. A little parakeet came to visit my bird cache. I named her Letty. One day, she didn't return. I miss you, so long Letty, goodbye.

Funny, how little things like this become a part of our lives. Do we select the ones we want? Or, do **they** cling to us? Even now, at 83, the memory of them singing that sweet, sad song, so long ago, touches me.

Married Up

Mother was a beautiful young lady, raised in the Episcopal Church. I have a memoir, charmingly written by Mom describing her trip from New York to California in 1921. She was a gifted lady. Daddy admired and loved Mother. He was proud of her. I think he knew he had "married up". Maybe bringing her down through those drunken binges bolstered his ego. Never thought of that before.

Marrying my Dad moderated her talent and verve. However, she stuck with him — for better or worse, as the saying goes.

We Knew We Were Loved

In spite of the bizarre drinking rite of our parents, and my grudge with my Mother, both Cathie and I knew we were loved. Our Mother had qualities of intelligence, wit, and responsibility. Daddy was fun, athletic, a good worker and social. I hope we got some of the good qualities from each parent!

"Gammy, What Did You Want to Be"

My little Grand Daughter asked me what I had wanted to be when I was young. I replied, "A secretary but, if I had had more exposure, I would have made a really good attorney." I like law and the thinking that goes with it. However, at the time in the little town of Whittier, I had no connection to law. So, being a secretary sounded good to me. As long as I can remember, I have always liked to help others.

Life Codes

Some nameless essence convinced me that I could achieve any goal. I emerged from my Nest with:

1. Passion for Life
2. I could do whatever I wanted in a world wide open for me
3. Do my best
4. Pay my bills on time
5. My Childhood Daydream

    And, I'm mad at my Mother

Phase Two

Fledging

From Lovely to Hot and Dusty

We leave the kind, lovely little community – "a Church on every corner" – of Whittier and move to the hot, dusty town of Bakersfield. Daddy drilled a well there and his work came first. Daddy brought a strange, half bunkhouse from an oil site to our acre of land. This was to be our home for four years.

Mother was stoically unhappy in Bakersfield. Collapsed on the couch with a wet washcloth on her head, Mother soaked in the misty waves of the swamp cooler Daddy had built.

Our Own Games

My sister and I had few toys. We devised our own games, which included digging a hole, filling it with water and sitting in it to cool off! We used the keys on a saxophone as a typewriter and played secretary; put a net across the dining room table and played ping pong. We wiled away our days in the sweltering town of Bakersfield from ages of nine to twelve.

In the Closet

I was preoccupied with my approaching puberty. I remember my thighs ballooning. I didn't like that. I loved being slim, agile and athletic. One time, I was hiding in the closet trying to provide for beginning female needs when my sister Marilyn opened the door to reveal me, mortified, with shame. I don't know why I was humiliated and self-conscious. I just was.

Marilyn

Our older sister Marilyn was high school queen and fascinated with the boys going off to World War II. And so were we as we watched her put color on her legs to duplicate stockings and pile her hair high in a stylish pompadour.

Junior High Times

I learned to read music and play the saxophone, E flat alto, for four years. This was a nurturing experience, which I enjoyed. I watched the conductor, came in on time and became part of our orchestra and band. I was an outstanding, award-winning athlete at our Washington Junior High. This ability garnered attention and approval from fellow students. We had a teacher who was enthralled with romance. Every Wednesday noon she played a waltz — *It's Three O'clock in the Morning* — as she tried to teach embarrassed eighth graders to dance.

The Dust Bowl

The poor folks from the Dust Bowl poured into Bakersfield. One blond, barefooted girl picked on me. I told Mother. She went right down to that school and gave them the what for! I had many times observed Mother shielding Cathie! But, me? It was my turn. I cherish her efforts on my behalf. I felt protected. The blond girl from the Dust Bowl was very nice to me after that.

A Party

I wanted to have a party for my eighth grade friends. My parents served hot dogs, ice cream and cokes. We had a great time. Mom and Dad had difficulty chaperoning the wild Bakersfield kids and were mortified that some of the twelve year olds brought liquor. The kids wanted me to have another party! Mom and Dad said, "Never again!" Life's politics learned early.

Back to Whittier

Bakersfield was a wild place compared to sweet, green Whittier. I loved Whittier and her gentle people. Whittier, Whittier, a town founded by Quakers, happily nurturing a small, Liberal Arts College and a soon to be President of the United States.

Still Friends

Cathie and I crashed onto the high school scene and instantly became popular and welcomed. Those four years in that school were a blessing for me. The kids were nice and kind, the school was supportive and nurturing. I had a wonderful circle of friends. We still correspond and, once or twice a year, get together for lunches.

Miss King

Academically, I got B's and A's without studying. I was there to "have fun"! There was one class I loved, a teacher I adored and that was Miss Ethyl King. She lived English Literature. She loved it and her glowing enthusiasm broke right into my heart. I treasured the beautiful writings to which she introduced us, especially Shakespeare. I still can recite lines from Macbeth, *"Is this a dagger which I see before me – the handle toward my hand?"* An interesting person in my class was Ed Nixon. Who knew that his brother would one day be President of the United States? Possibly, my love of writing now comes from this early experience under Miss King's inspired instruction. You teachers have influence far greater than you know. I wish so that you were reimbursed financially commensurate with your abilities to inspire the best in your students.

Learning to Kiss

Some of the freshman girls wanted to learn to kiss. Joan Kirkwood's brother Jack, a few years older than we, tried to teach us. Finally, we caught on. It *is* rather a strange thing when you think about it. But we knew it was important and we should learn to do it!! When we went out, we usually parked across the street and sat in the car and did what we called, "neck". It meant lots and lots of kissing and enjoying the boys getting all hot and bothered. Many times Mother flicked our porch light off and on. That meant, "Come in the house right now!"

Our Friends

In addition to boy friends as sweethearts, there were many really nice boys that were our friends and came over often. Our parents welcomed the young people into our home and were great parents during the high school years.

Fights Dwindle

Mom and Dad seemed to have got over their zeal for passionate fights – settled down to just drink and retire to bed. We did sometimes have to handle Mother. We had a scheme: I would visit with her in the bedroom while Cathie's date came to pick her up – and visa versa.

On to Victory

My senior year, I was Student Body Song leader along with four other girls. We had a blast! I was right at home In front of the crowd at every game. Our 1948 class was outstanding, capturing All-State awards in Basketball and Water Polo. We are celebrating a Brunch this year with 50 fellow graduates.

The Huntington Beach Hop

There were no rock bands, no Beetles. We didn't jump up and down, twist or shake our "booties". We did the slow dance, the swing, the New Yorker, the Balboa and the Lindy. We did adore our music: Frank Sinatra, Nat King Cole, Stan Kenton, Glenn Miller, Frankie Laine, Les Paul, and June Christy. When I was a junior, two fellows from Huntington Beach came to Whittier High: Eddie Brown and Bob Sowers. Eddie was darling and a great dancer. The Huntington Beach crowd had a special dance called the HB Hop. It was intricate but I learned to do it and Eddie and I danced and danced. We had great fun at dances and at the beach.

The Place to Be

We spent Easter Week at Balboa Island, a darling little place in Newport Beach. Our Easter dresses were bathing suits and we welcomed the exchange. We lay out on the sand to get tan, swam in the bay, and went to the Fun Zone on the ferry. Many of Southern California's high school students were there. It was the place to be.

Good Job, Mom!

Every day, when we were girls, Mother took us to the Whittier High Pool for swimming lessons. And, swim, we did. I broke the record for freestyle in our Whittier High pool and, for a time, was the fastest girl swimmer in Whittier. During the summer, any weekend we could get a ride, we went to the Beach – Huntington Beach. I loved riding the waves and, one time, went off the 33-foot pier – still remember that thrill!

Boys

I discovered them and they discovered me. I had many boyfriends, beginning my freshman year with fellow swimmer Charlie Stevenson. Charlie, Bob and I entered a Three MAN medley. I swam freestyle; Charlie swam butterfly and Bob back. We placed first in the Whittier Swim Meet!

Modeling

One of my dear friends was Joanne Owens. She and her brother Dick were amazing dancers – show type dancers. They had an early TV show called ***Teen Time.*** They asked me to model on the show, which I did a few times. I also performed in a few local modeling shows. I wasn't really very interested and made no efforts to continue in that venture.

Phase Three

Oh, Oh

Oh, Oh

After High School

After high school, I was challenged with choosing my next step. My Whittier life had been settled, sweet and kind. I was raised to welcome college. I considered going to UCLA. However, I had never been there and had no guidance about the procedures to attend a large university. Many of my girlfriends were going to a new school Mt. San Antonio College. It was about a half an hour from Whittier. So, the six of us bundled into the car and cast our lots on Mt. Sac.

A Good Choice

We had great fun!! I don't remember any classes of interest – oh, yes, business class in which I received an A. It was so easy. I should have got a hint from that. I took an IQ test there and for the first time realized I had a brain!! Not a genius, but close enough to file it in my memory bank.

Peggy, Irene and I were song leaders at Mt. Sac for two years!

First Love

It was there at Mt. San Antonio College where I met my first serious beau Tommy Lloy, handsome, athletic end on the football team. Tommy and I dated and were truly in love. We got along great, both loved sports, outdoors, horses, hunting. He was balanced and kind, honest and open. He gave me a ring. We became engaged and had an engagement party.

The Conflict Emerges

I don't remember what happened to set my *Conflict* off or why, but, somehow, some way, for some reason, I became angry and frustrated, took the ring off and threw it on the ground. I am ashamed of myself for doing that.

We were on and off after that. I was too unstable to treasure a committed relationship. At the time, I didn't realize I had a problem!

"You Are Loved"

I talk to Tommy now every once in a while. He just called a few days ago. He is 86 and feeling the effects. Tommy, his wife and I had breakfast together in Balboa. I've apologized to him for being so irrational in our young life. He has two boys and a girl; I have two boys and a girl. His daughter's name is Jeralyn; my daughter's name is Jerilee. I have no doubt that he was a perfect mate for me. He knows. I know. How many lives have been damaged with the twisted characteristics of my *Conflict*?

The Polo Field

Sister Marilyn and husband Tommy with their two little boys were living in Carpentaria at the Santa Barbara Polo Field. Tommy received a scholarship and acquired a part-time job exercising polo ponies. They settled in a little trailer in back of one of the barns. They invited me to come for a visit. I was in between semesters at Mt. Sac and happily joined them at the Polo Field.

Heaven

The Polo Field was heaven for me. I had planned to stay two weeks and stayed two months! I have always loved horses. Polo season was on and polo players were there from all over the United States. Each player had a string of about eight horses. Polo was played on Saturday and Sunday. I became friends with one of the grooms, helped him care for the horses and exercised the polo ponies. I took them out on the track, riding one, leading two on one side and one on the other, galloping round and round, conditioning them for the demanding competition of polo. Occasionally, I took sorrel mare Bunoka to the ocean to ride along the shore. What absolute heaven!

Freedom is riding my sorrel mare along
the sponge plump sand on the Santa Barbara Coast

No Girls on the Track!

To add to the wonder, Johnny Hulseman and I became pals. John's family owned the Solo Paper Cup Company. At the time and in those days, I allotted no credibility to inheritance or financial position. Johnny and I rode, went to parties, visited and had a good time. We planned to go to Jackson Hole, Wyoming and work at John Wert's (one of the players) hotel for the summer. Johnny's dad was concerned about our friendship, not wanting us to become really serious. As he was very influential with the Santa Barbara Polo Club, they supported his request and ruled that no females could ride on the track. I was the only girl that ever rode on the track. If I couldn't ride, I wanted to go back to Whittier. I had been there two months. It was one of the most beautiful times of my life.

I Regret That!

Johnny came to Whittier to see me. I got Johnny a date with one of my girl friends and really didn't even see him. Writing this now, I regret that!!

Aloha

Another friend at the Polo Field was Bobby Smith, a fine horseman. His Dad Bob Smith Sr. was a seven-goal polo player, the highest ranked at Santa Barbara. Bobby took a string of polo ponies to Hawaii and played polo there. He wanted me to come over.

"You Can Haze for Me"

After returning to Whittier, I became reinvolved with Tommy Lloy and, naturally, a new flame, Harry Floyd, another horseman, a Champion Bareback Rider. Harry had a beautiful little Quarter Horse from the King Ranch in Texas, *Joker Al*. Harry proposed, saying, "I'll get a little ranch in Fontana where I can practice bulldogging – and you can haze for me." Every time I see the name Fontana, I think of this!

Goodbye, Tommy Lloy

Tommy Lloy retired from his many years service with the Los Angeles Fire Department. He and his lovely wife live in Laguna Niguel, an elegant region of Newport Beach, California. Last time I saw him, he reminded me, "Your Mother thought I wasn't good enough for her precious princess."

Phase Four

Bewildered

Bewildered

Dropping Like Flies

My girl friends were dropping like flies to Mendelssohn's March. My sister, my pal, my friend Cathie married her college boyfriend. I supposed marriage should be my next step.

Enter Tommy McCaron. Tommy McCaron was what today's kids would call *cool*. He was handsome, smooth, a great tennis player and a wonderful dancer. His family had a business. He knew how to play bridge and was easy and casual to be with. We dated. So, when Tommy McCaron asked me to marry him, I said "Yes."

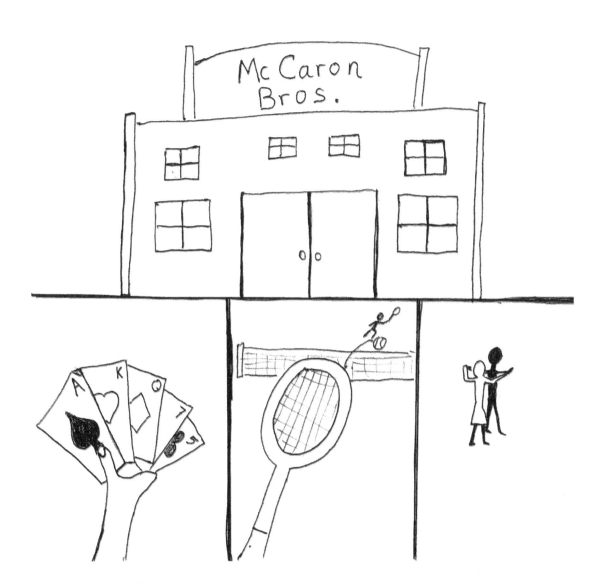

Nine Months

At the time, he worked for his dad in the family's manufacturing business. I wrongly assumed that would be his life career. It followed that he pursued many jobs in the year we were married. We lived in a little house in Baldwin Park, a small town close to Whittier. We moved to an apartment in South Pasadena and Tommy got a job driving a Coca Cola truck. He and I modeled for some Goodrich Tire ads. Our next move was to my Aunt Laura's ranch in Fullerton where we lived in an apartment in her back yard. Nine months and six days after our wedding, baby Girl McCaron was born in Whittier.

My Baby Girl

Alas, I broke my leg on the delivery table. I had no information regarding the birth event, no preparation for the experience of delivery. In those days, they strapped you onto the table. I pulled so hard the doctor heard a snap. It wasn't the straps. It was my bone. I came out of the hospital with my baby and a cast on my leg. We went back home to Whittier where Baby Jerilee and I stayed with Mother until my leg healed.

I Love Lucy

Tommy and I moved again, this time to Seal Beach. He got a job at a men's clothing store. I was restless. I painted the living room green, watched *I Love Lucy* and flirted with one of Tommy's friends. I got a job at one of the large airplane businesses in Long Beach. I think I was filing or typing. It was boring. I was bored. Tommy was a kind, sweet man. I managed to get him into fights with me. We began arguing. I self-satisfyingly concluded, "Marriage isn't supposed to be like this." and explored ways to get out of this situation.

"Let's Go Swimming"

I received a call from Marilyn and Tommy Gallon. Tom had started a swim school. Business was booming. They needed another teacher. They invited me to come to Bakersfield and teach swimming. When my little baby was a year old, I packed up and left Tommy – without looking back – to go to Bakersfield.

Shallow, Thoughtless and Foolish!

Tommy's mother, who had always been kind to me, said, "Honey, if you ever need anything, don't hesitate to ask. We'll be glad to help." How disgusted I am with my willful, selfish, response, "I don't need any help from you."

I went blithely on without tear or regret – so shallow, thoughtless and foolish. I took Jerilee with me everywhere I went. Thank God I had enough of a mothering instinct to keep her close.

So Sorry – Please Forgive Me

Years later, I apologized and asked her and Tommy to forgive me. How ashamed I was and am for these words, and for depriving Jeri of her loving and caring paternal family. It didn't help when Tommy's daughter told me he said at his last, "She was the love of my life." So inviting to begin rash, headstrong steps that reap a harvest of pain and anguish for years and deprive children and grandchildren of their birthright.

Wedding Number one and a Half — a wedding I don't count.

I don't know if I'll include this. It is a "marriage" I don't "count". Brother-in-law Tommy had a friend Vern Tucker who was a rather settled, stable type guy. He courted me while I was at Tom and Marilyn's. I suspicioned I was too radical and foolish and thought, 'Maybe, if I married this guy, I will become a mature person.' So, with this thought and no love, I married Vern. He was kind, sweet and gentle with Jerilee. I liked that. After nine months of this boring arrangement, that was over.

Let's Go Skiing

I loved sports. At this time, skiing was big on my ledger. I joined the Bakersfield Ski Club where I met Phil Zander, geologist for Shell Oil. We spent some time together. He was a very nice guy who was a graduate of Stanford. Phil took me to meet his mother in Palo Alto. The Ski Club went to Sun Valley, Idaho. I was an amateur. Phil, a splendid skier, took me up on what I later learned was a **black diamond** run. It was steep! I was mortified, cried and side slipped the entire time down. I was miffed with Phil after that experience.

Another friend was Yves Pajot who carefully explained to me that Yves was a male name in his hometown of Brussels, Belgium. Yves spoke French, English and Flemish and was a gentleman, handsome and great skier.

I had a brief friendship with Ted Johnson, a somewhat famous skier whose remarkable picture was on Sports Illustrated. Ted was handsome, sophisticated (compared to me!) and an amazing skier. He did teach me to make a Hawaiian o'deruve. Ted didn't take time to offer the usual proposal. He was on the run.

Besieged With Proposals

Almost all of these very interesting individuals invited me to be a life-long partner. I was besieged with proposals and was overwhelmed with the friendship of interesting and attractive men.

And, then, I met Freddy Goldberg.

Phase Five

Freddy Goldberg

Freddy Goldberg

Fred Goldberg

Jeri and I lived in a little apartment on Loma Linda Lane in Bakersfield. I now had that secretarial job! For five years I worked for Easton & Sacre, Petroleum Engineers in Bakersfield. I loved my job. I've always liked to work. Also, since my Dad was in the oil business, the phrases and aspirations of oil seekers were familiar and interesting to me.

Next door lived an artist, Eve Moore. We were friends. She painted a beautiful portrait of Mary Magdalene kneeling at the Cross. I knew nothing about Mary Magdalene or the Cross but I knew that was a beautiful painting. If anyone knows where it might be, I would cherish having that painting.

At the Pool

Jerilee and I were at the local gathering place, a large swimming pool. There he was, this adorable guy who flirted with me. I flirted back and we began a passionate love affair for some five years. I was madly in love with Fred. We married, quickly had our first child Richard. A year and half later, we welcomed our next boy Adam.

We lived a few blocks from the Temple. I studied with the Rabbi, and learned to interpret Hebrew phonetically without understanding the meaning. That was the custom in the Temple wherein the Jews could pronounce the words but did not understand their meaning. Rabbi Kolatch said I was the smartest person he had ever instructed. I'm not sure how that information affected me however I do remember it! I also remember and miss the delicious Jewish food.

Father Fred

I learned a lot about being a parent from Fred. When my sister and I misbehaved as children, Mother said, "Go to the lemon tree and get a switch." We got the skimpiest ones we could find. In we came, heads bowed, hearts thumping with fear as Mother thrashed our legs with the lemon tree switch.

I watched Fred with the boys. He was gentle and kind. I never remember him hitting or spanking them – even when they, playing Batman and Robin, cut the top of the convertible or when Richard broke the large plate glass window with a hammer. He was a superb father to the young boys.

A Remarkable Lady

Richard and Adam went to a preschool directed by a gifted lady Dorothy Hewes. As it was a parent participation school, I assisted a few days a week. I searched Ms. Dorothy like a hawk. She had a unique way with the children. I sensed her genius as she encouraged the children to explore, create, grow and express. I got it!! Through the **miracle of modeling**, her gift was wrapped and packaged onto me. I will ever be grateful for this wonderful experience.

"Pump Gas?"

Fred was working for his Dad in the Delano grape business of Irving Goldberg and Sons, the largest fruit packers in Delano and the eighth largest in the world. His Dad decided to quit the business.

This talented person, with many skills and abilities, had not been prepared emotionally or academically to do anything other than work for his Dad in the packing shed. He was bummed and spent the days lying on the couch.

I said, "Freddy, why don't you go get a job?"

Fred replied, "What do you want me to do, pump gas?"

My Conflict Erupts

Rather than understanding, being kind, supportive, and helpful, I was antagonistic, judgmental and critical. I protested by returning to my secretarial skills to work for petroleum geologists.

We moved from our darling magazine-cover home into a tract house. Things went from bad to worse. We argued a lot. That's all I knew how to do — not listen, not care — just argue. In the kitchen in a hot (we kept our passion on all fronts) argument, he pushed me. That did it for me.

Forget About It

I hated to leave Fred. After the truck was packed, we were in the yard, preparing to leave.

"Fred, I will go to counseling if you will."

"Who do you want to see?"

"David Hewes."

"If you go to that jerk, forget about it."

(Incidentally, everyone in Bakersfield who went to Hewes for counseling that I know of got divorced.)

I Forgot About It!

I forgot about it and, with Jeri, Richard and Adam, went up to Albany to attend the University of California, Berkeley. School was hard. Competition was stiff. I had three kids at home. I knew no one. The Free Speech Movement was in full force with Joan Baez and Mario Salvio (whatever happened to him?) performing daily.

I did go out with one man during this time. All I remember of him is his name, Dr. John. He was a research specialist and told me he knew more about the blood pressure of the unborn fetus than anyone in the world. I remember this and not his last name! He was kind to the kids. He came to visit me in Bakersfield and I, as the saying now is, shined him on. Fred wrote a touching letter. Adam read it as a grown-up and said it was hard to believe his Dad had written it — it was so tender, intelligent, thoughtful and loving.

Called It Quits

I made it through the first semester and, in the middle of the second, I called it quits and returned to Bakersfield. Other than failed marriages, it's the only time I remember "giving up". During the process of decision-making, I wandered into a church and talked with the Pastor. I don't know what church it was. The Pastor didn't introduce me to Jesus. He just told me to go back to my husband in Bakersfield.

Back to Bakersfield

Fred proposed to me again and wanted to get back together. We went down to LA and stayed at a nice hotel. He bought me a dress and festooned the room with flowers. Of course, by this time, I had another boyfriend Dan Shippey who resembled his cousin Glen Campbell. Dan was just a guy, nice, kind, friendly and sweet with the children.

I asked Fred to wait three days while I thought it over. I told him "No." He was furious. He picked up my large glass water bottle and slammed it to the ground, accusing, "You're going with that mechanic."

Yes? No. Yes? No.

When I wanted to go back with Fred, he wasn't willing. When he wanted to get together with me, I wasn't willing. The last time I attempted to reconcile, I went to Hermosillo where he was supervising a grape business. I remember helping him with his office where a little girl told me the name of the nail – I was hanging pictures – *un clavo*. Strange how some memories cling.

At the Airport

At this time Freddy was dating a beautiful girl Adriana Lopez. I thought I could win him back. No. He dropped me off at the airport and left. I was broken hearted and sad to my depths. As I was walking on the tarmac to enter the plane, suddenly, I heard Fred's voice, "Marj". I looked up. He had returned and was in the crowd of those saying goodbye to the passengers. I continued and got on the plane. This, I think, was the saddest day of my life as I flew back to the hot, dusty town of Bakersfield, alone.

Don and Betty's

Many years later, I was visiting Fred's brother Don and wife Betty at their home. Just chatting away. Suddenly, when mentioning Fred, from deeper than deep, within my being streamed wrenching tears. I sobbed with my whole heart. They watched, understanding with a tender wisdom. I had yet to learn marriage roots were intertwined and didn't disappear with the apparent ease of the separation and divorce. I wonder how many others have suffered this sad, sad discovery?

A Broken Communication

I was deeply in love with Fred.
I had no commitment to an enduring relationship.
I hadn't learned to love.
I convinced myself that the vow didn't matter.
I hardened my heart.
And built a wall with thoughts and beliefs to
Pretend I was right.
A home broken.
A father denied.
Sons without their Father
For years I had dreams.
For years I had anxious dreams – seeking connection.

They left to call him to the phone.
They never returned. He never came.
The line would break.
Sometimes, the phone wouldn't ring.
Dream after dream – a broken communication.
Year after year.

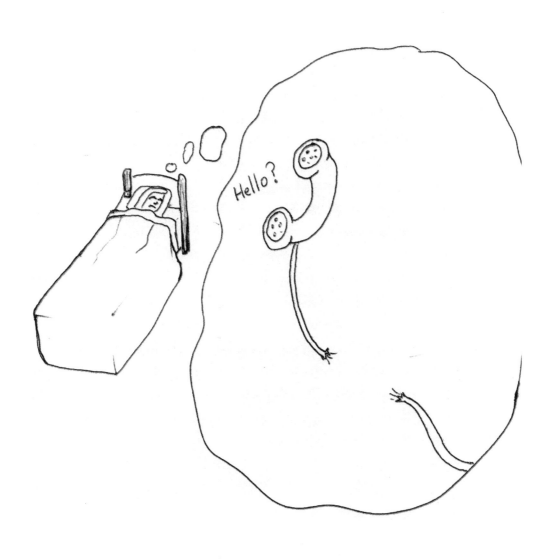

Rennie and Grant's Bar Mitzvah

I went to Rennie and Grant's Bar Mitzvah.
The first time I had seen Fred in 10 years.
The pain in his face.
The hurt mouth.
The flight of tender youth.
The loss of joy.
It was all there to read in his face.
Like words in a book.

Fred and I never signed the divorce papers.
In front of my desk, right now, is a card he wrote and
one I kept all these years.

All my love all my life
Your husband today, tomorrow and always.
                    Fred

I wonder if he remembers writing that?? I wonder if I'll
include that in this Book? I've written this many times,
working on this book for you. It still brings tears to my
eyes and a wince to my heart.

Phase Six

Santa Cruz

Santa Cruz

99th Percentile!

I continued classes at Bakersfield College and Fresno State Extension in Bakersfield. While taking an examination, I learned I scored in 99th percentile in Psychological Foundations of Education. I believe this skill comes directly through the magical aperture shared by my Mystical Daydream and Dorothy Hewes, the pre-school teacher I observed when the children were young.

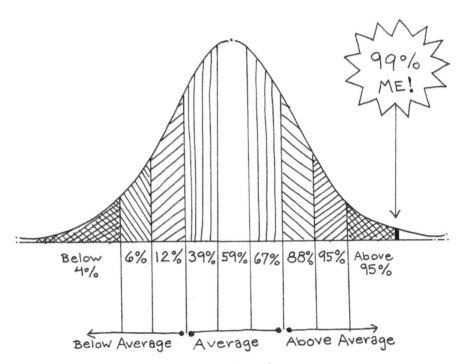

Percentile Score
Psychological Foundations
of Education

A Brand New Teaching Job

A brand new teaching job opened in Wasco – Head Start. No prior program, no one knew much about it. I knew I did. I went up to Wasco, some 30 minutes from Bakersfield and applied for the job. I had no training, no early childhood education courses. I just knew I knew how to do it. I interviewed with the Education Director and got the job.

A Sweet Time

For three years, I taught pre school with two wonderful aides: Alice and Vera. We had two classes, one with children of Mexican descent and one with children of African descent. The first year was hard. Some of the things I thought I knew would work didn't. Ah, but the second and third years were pure gold. Little was pre-set or given. We had a marvelous, creative time, designing our program. It was wonderful. I loved it.

Caesar Needed to Rest

I don't remember where I met Marshall Ganz but we became friends. I do remember his Dad was a Rabbi in Bakersfield. Marshall, a very gifted guy, was working with the farmworkers who were trying to form a union in order to extract additional wages from the landowners. Actually, the way it worked (and probably still does) is the farm workers had a boss who negotiated with the landowners; then, he hired and paid the workers. Anyway, Marshall called one day and said Caesar (Chavez) was really tired and could he come over to my place and rest (21st and B in Bakersfield). I said "Sure," so Caesar came over, rested on our couch and took a nap. Caesar was a small man, kind, gentle and polite. Mostly, he was tired.

The Farmworkers and the Sox

Marshall said, "Well, the name of the Union is UFOC! United Farmworkers Organizing Committee." I'm not sure he liked that name. The farmworkers were marching to Sacramento, lead by Caesar, Dolores Huerta and Marshall. He called and asked me to send several dozen pairs of sox. The farmworkers had sore feet. Of course, I purchased and sent the sox. Marshall returned to education and is now a professor at the Kennedy School of Business at Harvard and still organizing.

A Little Flower

At this stage, harkening to the times, I was very rebellious, and painted a little flower on my VW. Wasco was segregated. With Alice and Vera, we broke the color barrier. I applied for an Experienced Teaching Fellowship in Early Childhood Education. I'm sure my principal was supportive because he wanted to purge his staff from my influence. I was nonconformist and customarily proposed creative changes in our school's education system. That always causes problems for any principal.

Teaching Fellowship

I was accepted and received the Fellowship. This time we travelled to Pacifica. I attended San Francisco State for eleven months. I met some lovely friends, including Judy Hubner who became and still is a lifelong friend. Another friend was David Smith, Founder and Director of the Haight-Ashbury Free Medical Clinic. After eleven months, I received the Master's Degree.

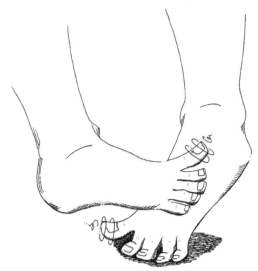

Restrictions

I was offered funding to continue in a PhD program. I was resentful of the many requirements, often boring to me, in the Master's Program. Rather than following **my** inspirations, they wanted the student to follow **their** inspirations.

One of my instructors condescendingly asked, "Johana (I am now using my middle name.), how do you know how to do that?" "Miss Smith, I know how to do that like I know how to move my big toe."

Back to Bakersfield? Not This Time

After being in and around the sophistication of San Francisco, the return to Bakersfield sounded very dreary to me.

From this time on, very unusual, strange, extraordinary happenings happened.

Unusual Happening Number One – "We Want You to Have It"

One of my Fellows said his Aunt had a house in Aptos, California, that they wanted to rent. "I can only pay $300 a month." Ken talked with his Aunt who said, "Great, come down and look at the place. We want you to have it." The house was one block from the ocean. It was perfect. We rented it and moved to Aptos, a beautiful little slice of Santa Cruz in California.

The Brown Trailer

At the end of our year in the beach house, they wanted the house back! A deep-seated, primitive yearning pressured me to make soap, wear long dresses, create and paint little beads. I longed to live with nature, not surrounded or confined to a house or a building. For a few days, Adam and I settled on Black's Beach. It was all glory, with the ocean and sun coming and going. My teaching partner Bob Rowbear Lowman found an old trailer, which he moved to the back two acres of Marsha Carr's, one of our fellow teachers in the Santa Cruz Free School. Outside of our trailer was a gorgeous 250-acre bird sanctuary next to Twin Lakes. We loved it. We rode our horses, planted a garden and cuddled our pet duck Dorothy. Richard, who by nature was more traditional than Ad or I, didn't like living in a funky trailer.

The Santa Cruz Free School

The Sixties produced a group dismayed with traditional education. We gathered and formed the Santa Cruz Community Free School. Bob Rowbear Lowman was my partner and we had about 13 kids. His parents had a nice house in the Aptos hills and most of our activities were there. We designed our learning program. The kids created their own book, which sold out. We were living it!

More Studies

I continued my self-designed, postgraduate education. I was interested in emotion and communication and selected courses/experiences to advance my training. I went to Esalen Institute at Big Sur, California where I met and "worked" with Fritz Perls, founder of Gestalt Therapy. I also attended several sessions of EST – Erheardt Seminar Training – all the rage to get in touch with one's emotions. I studied: Love, Acceptance and Openness; Massage; The Primal Scream; Anger Release; I'm Okay, You're Okay; Rolfing; Transactional Analysis; and Advanced Drug and Alcohol Training at the University of California, Santa Cruz.

Around 1968 – about 38 years of age

I was seeking, looking, searching. Trying to find something that I didn't know what I was looking for. Like a blind person in a swampy forest, pushing fronds and branches aside, going off on wild trails, thinking, "Ah, this is the way." Really, just passionately groping and impulsing my way through life. After going through many friends, boy friends and husbands, racking through every psychological theory of the age, I, as the saying goes, reached the end of my rope. What was left?

Happening Number Two – "Help"

You know my religious background: not saying the Lord's Prayer, Christmas Carols, Daddy's Thanksgiving Prayer. We lived on a hill on Treasure Island in Rio Del Mar. Realizing I had depleted all areas of my search, I knew I was lost. Some Thing implored me to kneel, weeping. I raised my arms, imploring some Thing to help me. I didn't know what I wanted the Help to do but just knew it was some Thing somewhere.

Helping Parents

I did know that I wanted to help people – to make their lives better. Through my studies at San Francisco State and especially my home study of Anthony, I observed that the people that needed help were parents. Back to training. I enrolled in Parent Effectiveness Training Program, designed to help the enrollees teach parents parenting skills.

Helping Trumps Fear

I have always been agonizingly petrified when speaking in front of other adults. In high school, on my report day, I made some excuse to stay home in an effort to postpone the misery. In the PET training, the students were assigned to present an example class. The desire to help others trumped fear. I stepped out – like catching the wave at the swell, just before the curl. It was great. No fear. Just excitement and the thrill of knowing I could do it.

Silverbelle

We lived in the country in Aptos on Freedom Boulevard on seven acres. I had seen a beautiful little white Welsh pony and stopped to ask the owner about buying her. He said "No." Five years later, some Thing moved me to ask again. He said, "Yes." Silverbelle became ours. I loved her forever. At 19, when the vet said, "This mare is terminal." I cried like a baby. I have a picture of her here now. Dear Silverbelle, I do hope horses are in heaven.

Happening Number Three – No More Cigarettes

For years I had smoked about seven cigarettes a day. I was out running when a little voice said, "You're killing your body with the cigarettes." I thought, "Oh my gosh. What is that?" I decided to follow the little voice and quit smoking; always believing I could quit anytime I chose. I did pretty well for about two days and then the – what? Desire? Lust? Want? came. I hopped in my blue V-Dub, went to the liquor store and bought a pack of cigarettes. I smoked the entire pack that night, and disgustedly said to myself, "You junky!"

No Believer

Upon awakening the next day, I remember this and the wonder feeling of it, I no longer had any desire to smoke. I never smoked another cigarette. I didn't realize at the time – since I had no Believer! – that it was God who freed me from the smoking habit.

Phase Seven

The Voice in the Volkswagen

The Voice in the Volkswagen

I Become a Teacher!

Armed with these insights:

A   Emotions come and go.
   They color life with fun.
B. Crying is good. It releases pain and sadness.
C. Forcing not to cry, using anger and threats, harms the child.
D.   Listening solves most problems.

The Teacher set out to transform the world through teaching parents and individuals these basic concepts.

Warm, Rosy Glow

The Teacher loved teaching the class. The practice of listening skills was an important class activity. A warm rosy glow came over the students as they listened carefully to one another to practice this skill. We sat, soaking it in. One student remarked, "That's the Holy Spirit." I said nothing. Ignorant as to what the Holy Spirit was, I thought to myself, "Humph, that's Love."

The Thing Was Prowling After Me!

I was on the prowl, searching for something and not knowing what it was. Is there a word for that? Probing? Inspecting? Examining? Searching? Questioning? Inquiring? Exploratory Action? That's it! EXPLORATORY ACTION for the purpose of discovery, the process of finding some Thing, a Thing I knew not what.

Little did I know that while I was rummaging after that Thing, that Thing was prowling after me!

Meditation

That might be It. Sitting quietly for 20 minutes, focusing on that third eye place almost in the center of the forehead. Up in the morning at 4:00. Out on the blanket to meditate in the early morning prana. That was good.

Breathing

Oh yes. Don't forget breathing. Low, in the abdomen, softly, quietly, In - count 4 - hold - count 4 - out – count 4, etc. etc.

Sufi Dancing

We had such great fun Sufi dancing. The swaying and bowing were sweet.

Study

Loved Kahil Kibran's *The Prophet*; Martin Buber's *Thou and I*. Very impressive. Transforming situations through serving. Wow! Zen Buddhism – They might have something here. Tried to read my Grandmother's Bible. Didn't understand a word!

Happening Four ~ The Voice in the Volkswagen

I read an Eastern Book about the Bright Light. Oh, that sounded good.

I wanted that Bright Light. As I meditated, concentrating on that center of my forehead, in my little blue Volkswagen behind our cabin in Ben Lomond, I said over and over "Let me see the Bright Light. Let me see the Bright Light."

I kept saying that as I meditated and then a voice said, "**Forget about the Bright Light and love me.**" Was I surprised! "**Forget about the Bright Light and love me.**" Golly. What does that mean and who is talking to me??? Good Heavens.

Happening Five – The Bright Light

This night after hearing the voice saying "Forget about the Bright Light and Love Me", I came into my little cabin in Ben Lomond in the hills above Santa Cruz. The room was rough-hewn wood and across the back was a loft. As was my usual exercise, I wrapped my fingers around the frame and eased down. Suddenly, immediately, an immense Bright Light totally filled my vision – my everything. A Light so bright, exceedingly bright – I cannot convey to you how bright that light was. It was totally, totally, comprehensively bright. I couldn't see. It blinded me. I released my hold on the frame, staggered backward and tumbled onto the couch. My legs and body felt electrified. I knew I had seen the Bright Light and that the Voice had heard my request and answered it and I laughed with awe and joy.

Happening Six - Golden Streams

The next day after the Bright Light, I was sitting outside on our deck. I wore a small, yellow-diamond ring my mother had given me; the glint from the yellow diamond went all the way up to the Heavens. Around my arm and hand was a soft whitish aura I could visibly see, that moved when I moved. I was fascinated, watching the Golden Streams reaching to the sky all the way up, as far as I could see and the soft whitish aura that moved when I moved. I thought I would always see things this way. But I didn't. It was just that one day – after seeing the Bright Light.

Happening Seven – "My Name is John"

A few weeks later, I was walking along the street in Santa Cruz with my daughter Jerilee. We had been at the Old Catalyst (some of you will remember this) drinking coffee, visiting with the locals. Outside was a man sitting on a wide store sill, panhandling. He had the look of an alcoholic, disheveled hair, red face, and bleary eyes. We were waiting for the signal to change to cross the street to the car - yes, the little blue Volkswagen.

When I saw the man sitting on the sill, a profusion of thoughts hammered, "What is he doing there? Why isn't he out working? He shouldn't be drinking. He shouldn't be asking people for money. I don't like him being there. How disgusting."

"My Name is John"

At exactly this same instant, some Thing picked me up by the back of the neck like a mother cat picks up her baby and placed me beside the man. I slipped my hand into the pocket of my brown jacket, took out two quarters and gave them to the man, placing my hand on his shoulder, saying, "Sorry to see you so down and out, Brother."

"Sorry to see you so down and out, Brother!" Good night! You must be kidding! Where did those words come from? - Not from me with my negative, opinionated attitude. And I never called a stranger then or now or anyone "Brother" – ever!!

The man looked up at me with the eyes of an Angel, eyes I can never describe but will never forget. He took my hand in his - like a courtly gentleman - kissed my hand and said simply, "My name is John."

The Light Turned Green

When John looked at me with his angel eyes and kissed my hand, I was profoundly and deeply moved. I was changed. Some Thing happened. My hard, opinionated, I am always right heart had been ripped. I began sobbing. This all happened as Jerilee was waiting at the curb for the light to change. It turned green. We walked across the street. I cried for an hour.

I looked many times after for John. He was never there?

Happening Eight - Jesus Christ, Superstar - Friday Night

The play Jesus Christ, Superstar was being presented in the Harbor High School theatre. I have no idea why I wanted to go. I didn't like anything religious. I thought Jesus was a really nice guy and a model for human behavior. I believed Christians were namby-pamby hypocrites and that the Bible was a book of myth and history. No. I did not want to have any dealings with religion - Yuck!

But, there I was, drawn to this little play in this little theatre. I went alone, entered and sat down. Sometimes I wonder if this is my imagination? Will you believe me? I wonder. There was no one in the audience. People were at the door to give me a program. There were two pianists, many dancers, a full cast.

I was fascinated with Jesus. My eyes tracked every move. That was Friday night.

Jesus Christ, Superstar – Saturday Night -
The Show Must Go On – and on

The next night, I went again. Again, no audience. What gives? I stalked Jesus religiously. Once again, they performed the entire musical without an audience.

Topaz and the Potluck

I had a very dear friend. His name was Don Mills. He was kind, thoughtful and trying to be a hippy. To fit in with the Santa Cruz scene, Don changed his name to Topaz. If Topaz liked you, he reached in his pocket and meaningfully gave you a small, smooth stone.

One afternoon he asked me if I wanted to go to a church potluck. The adventuress said, "Sure." We went to a big red, brick church on High Street in Santa Cruz, the First Presbyterian Church.

The Fellowship Hall was a large room, filled with tables, laden with good food. A man greeted me and asked me what I did. I told him I taught Parenting and Communication Classes at Cabrillo College. He asked me if I would teach a class for the church. Of course, the crusader said, "Yes."*

Darn! Going to Church!

Every Sunday morning I taught the Class from 9 to 10. The students asked me to go to Church. I said "No." and made an excuse. One morning, Cathy Brunemer asked me; I meant to say my usual "No." and found myself saying, "Yes." Damn! Where did that "Yes" come from? So, into the hallowed sanctuary I went. I didn't want to go, but I did.

I didn't understand anything the Pastor said. I loved the singing and the music. I understood nothing about the Bible, about the Christian religion, about Jesus. Except Christmas carols, but I didn't understand them either. I did not know there was an Old and New Testament. I did not know what the Gospels were. I was Scripturally illiterate. And, I did not believe in sin.

The Rosy Net

I continued going to the Wednesday night potlucks. We had fun playing volleyball, visiting and going to Church on Sunday. This Wednesday night at the potluck, I was telling my tablemates about the play Jesus Christ Superstar. "They had two pianos and many dancers. I didn't like the part where Jesus was whipped."

Phillip, who sat to my right, searched intently then asked, "Who do you think Jesus is?"

I was swiftly enveloped by a fervent rosy glow. It seemed as though I were lifted up to the top of the ceiling. I felt disoriented and fearful. "What's happening? What's going on?" Phillip said, "That's the Holy Spirit. Do you want to receive Christ?"

I did not know what the "Holy Spirit" was. I did not know what "receive Christ," meant. But I knew one thing. Whatever It was that surrounded me with His Rosy Glow, my answer was "Yes, Oh Yes."

Capture Complete

I went with Phil to the Fireside Room and there, with weeping, I asked Jesus Christ to come into my heart. I was captured. I didn't want to be. I didn't understand any of the rituals or traditions. I didn't confess to sin (which I didn't believe in), I didn't know anything about the Cross and Jesus dying for us or being sent by God to redeem us. I knew nothing.

In Love With the Word

Phillip brought me a Bible the next day. The words that before were confusing and meaningless now soared through with meaning and wisdom. I studied and absorbed the Bible. I especially loved the book of Isaiah. Phillip and Carol Hill mentored me.

Filled

We were feeding the homeless. Another church group of youths came to help and play music. After, they asked, "Does anyone want to be prayed with to receive the Filling of the Spirit?" (Not a Presbyterian Sacrament) I was scared but I said, "I do."

We went into the Upper Room where they gathered around me and began praying. I felt timid and uncertain. And then, at a certain point, they encouraged me to – what can I say? Babble. I babbled and, little by little the new speech came to me. I was filled with the Spirit and spoke in the Heavenly Language. For seven years, I continued to attend the Red Brick Church and also went to different churches where I spoke in tongues, prophesied at the Assembly of God and journeyed through the Stages of the Cross at the Catholic Church.

One night, Carol Hill and a group were praying in the Fireside Room. Carol began speaking in tongues – Chinese tongues. And, I kid you not, her entire face changed and she looked Chinese! Am I losing you here? It actually happened!

Believe in Sin? Not me!

I didn't believe in sin. Therefore, I didn't, couldn't confess my sins. I didn't have any. After about a year, I got the point. Sin actually means, "missing the mark" so that if you're aiming at the bull's eye and hit the first ring next to it, you've sinned!! Good Golly! You can see why I didn't want to believe in sin! I thought if one had good intentions, it made everything all right. I had missed so many bull's eyes! It was agony to meet the wrongs and consider the pain I had dragged through life. Little by little, with Jesus securely in my heart, we trudged through it together, never more than I could bare, but - - -

The Spirit World

The enemy didn't like losing such a good warrior. He attacked me and, more than once, I "pled the blood" – on my knees, covering myself with the Blood of Christ and rebuking the Devil: "Be gone, in the name of Jesus!"

One day, it was given to me to see into the spirit world. I actually saw evil everywhere I looked. It was very ugly. I was frightened. I called Carol who said, "I'll get my Bible and be right over." She was a wonderful Spiritual Mother. Thank you, Carol

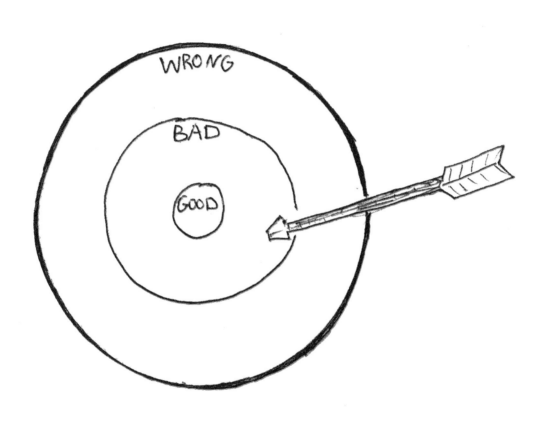

In Love With Phillip

Phillip and I were deeply drawn to one another. We separated for six months and still intensely wanted to be together. We were married in the Church. Immediately, peculiar things happened. The beauty and love we experienced disappeared, vanquished by hostility and confusion. The marriage was annulled. We married again, the same thing happened. That marriage also was annulled. This remains a Mystery.

My Household

Richard, one morning, was cooking. He felt very happy and out of this joy sprang, "Jesus, if you want to come into my heart, come in." He counts that as his day of Salvation. Adam was walking along the beach when he spied a Crucifix shining in the shore. He picked it up and brought it home. "Mom, I want to say that prayer you said about Jesus." Jerilee also soon invited the Lord into her life. All three children are living wholesome lives. So very grateful!

A Strange Prophecy

One time Phillip and I were in my place in Mt. Hermon, asking about our future. The Holy Spirit was strong. Phillip said, "Look at your face." I did. Looking in the mirror, I saw my face, white with a white halo around me. We received a message from the Lord. He said I was to marry someone like Rusty Garrison. I recognized this message to be an honor and recited the Magnificat.

Rusty was an honored man in our Church. He was intelligent, kind, knowledgeable and MARRIED! I interpreted the message to mean that God was going to change Phillip to become, not the young person he was, but a mature gentleman, like Rusty Garrison.

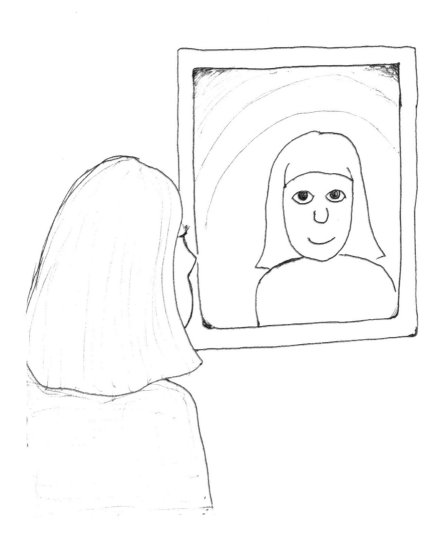

Phillip's Story – Kind Of

I will ever be grateful to Phillip and his gift of Evangelism for knowing how to "get" me!!!! Phillip told me he was strongly influenced to beseech God for my salvation. He was side by side with the Spirit as they prowled and stalked to bring me into the Kingdom.

Phillip became a Doctor of Pharmacology. He lives now in Los Gatos. We are still friends, in touch with one another.

Other Partners

One of the parents in my Watsonville class gave me a book entitled *Jesus as Teacher*. At the time, I wondered, "Why is she giving me this? Oh, well." I still have it! I was working with the Santa Cruz County Foster Parent Association. Little did I know, the entire group of some 23 persons was praying for me to meet the Savior.

Brown Faces – A New Gift

Another time, a group of African American women was meeting at Mt. Hermon. They invited me to come to their gathering. I did. As I entered the meeting room, I was startled to see the many dark faces. Oooh. As if planned, they gathered back to form a path and lead me to the front to sit with their honored speakers!

One lady began to speak:

"We got on the bus."

"Oh Yeah."

"There was a young boy there."

"Um Ummm."

And continued like that combining the speaker and the listeners in a spontaneous drama. At a certain moment, it changed from a lady telling a story to a beautiful melodious, heavenly rendition of a heart-changing allegory. What a blessing and privilege to be in their presence.

We sang and sang. I could feel the song in my chest, my bones – they kind of buzzed. Marion said to me, "I think you're getting the Spirit." They wanted me to speak. I did. I don't remember what I said.

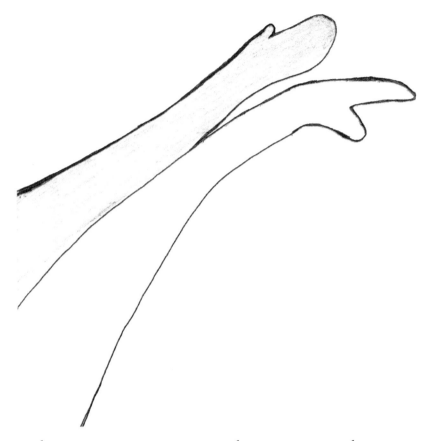

"When We Get to Heaven, This Won't Be There"

A beautiful girl came up to me and held her arm next to mine and said these never to be forgotten words: "When we get to Heaven, this won't be there."

Black Blood in Our Veins

I came home and told Richard and Adam that I thought we had Black Blood in our veins. Richard jumped up and down joyously saying, "I knew it. I knew it. That's why I can dance so well and Adam can play basketball." Go figure.

That's my story. And I'm sticking to it.

I Tried

After, I went to other black churches, hoping it would be the same. It wasn't.

When the Roll is Called Up Yonder

I became interested in Mom's spiritual history, knowing she was involved with the Episcopal Church as a youth and wondered, "Is she saved?" Driving back from GYE, full of the Spirit, I asked, "Will Moma be in Heaven?" A strange thing happened. Some Thing started in my bones. I didn't know what it was. It continued its way until it reached my song bank and out came: "When the Roll is Called Up Yonder, I'll be there."

Such a darling way to answer my question! Who would have thought of such a thing!???

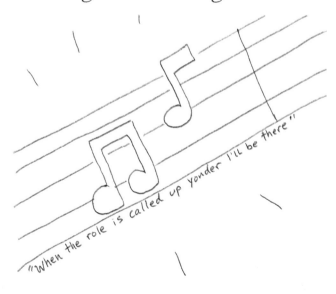

"When the role is called up yonder I'll be there"

Phase Eight
Stripped Bare

Stripped Bare

Stripped Bare

For years I had supported myself through teaching and counseling. SUDDENLY, the well went dry. My work with the Foster Parent Association was concluded, no classes at Cabrillo and no seminars. It all stopped. I stayed for a while with son Adam, setting my computer up in a closet!

Home With Elizabeth

One morning at Church, I met an elderly lady named Elizabeth. I absolutely fell in love with her and I guess she fell in love with me. She needed help. I had a job. For eight months, I lived with Elizabeth and cared for her. We went places together, walked on the track at Cabrillo, shopped, and lunched at the Tea Room in Capitola. It was a sweet time.

Elizabeth said, "I want to be excited about God like you are. How can I be?" "Well, Elizabeth, you can say the prayer I said. Do you want to do that?"

"Yes, I do."

Dear Lord Jesus, I invite you to come into my heart and be my Lord and my Savior.

"Is that all?" "Yep. That will do it."
Elizabeth said the prayer.

I loved being with Elizabeth and taking care of her; yet, I was uncertain about my life and my future. I remember asking her to adopt me!!

Black Bamboo

I cared for Elizabeth's plants, one of which was a very intriguing black bamboo. Wherever I've wandered after leaving Elizabeth's, I acquire a black bamboo in memory of her. Little things. Little things.

The Black Mercedes

One night, I beseeched God, questioning, "Oh God, what is to become of me?"

That night, I had a dream. I was on the top of a small mountain and there was a shiny, black, single-door Mercedes. God said it was for me.

Ruth and Obed

There was a man in the Church with whom I constantly agreed. We were both Elders and regularly on the same side in spiritual discussions in Session meetings. We were in a play together: **The Story of Ruth.** I played the part of Ruth who was a widow. Rusty played the part of Obed, a wealthy, kind businessman. Guess what? Obed rescues Ruth from poverty and marries her.

He asked me to teach a nine-month **Kerygma** class with him. "Doesn't Barbara (his wife) want to do it?" He said, "I asked her and she said 'No.'" And I said, "Yes, it will be fun." We met at the Tea Room in Capitola every Wednesday, going over our Class. Many times, Barbara went with us. I loved them both.

At the Tea Room

We met that next Wednesday. No Barbara. I sensed a strange ambiance on the loose and mentioned it. Rusty said, "I am in love with you."

OMG, what to do! I was dismayed!

Our Evangelism Committee went to Mills College to attend an Evangelism Seminar. Outside, away from the others, he asked, "If I were free to marry you, would you marry me?"

During the next few years, I thought a lot about my answer. I pondered and blurted out "Yes." If I said "No.", it would be a lie; if I said "Yes." who knew what would happen next?

What Happened Next

Rusty whisked off to Reno to establish residence and become free to marry me. The Church had a fit. We were both Elders, an important position in the Presbyterian Church. I was incredibly involved with Church. I taught classes, wrote and lead seminars and plays and continued to study the Bible. My grandson Laddy, age 10, and I painted the women's restroom. I poured my heart out as I tried to convince the Pastor and other Elders that I had not solicited this guy or tried to win him away from his wife. They didn't believe me. I was heart-broken.

"I'm Not Taking You Back"

After my unnerving visit with the Pastor and Elders of our Church, I arrived at Elizabeth's, sobbing my heart out. Elmer called from Reno. He repeatedly asked if he could come to get me. Finally, broken-hearted and weeping, I relented and said, "Yes."

He came. Leaving Santa Cruz, on the way up Highway 17, he put his hand on mine and said, "I'm not taking you back." The Pastor in Carson City, Nevada married us in the Presbyterian Church.

"It Won't Last Six Months"

I was devastated about the Church. I was wounded to think I had disappointed God and hurt Barbara whom I also loved. The Pastor said, "This won't last six months; he's ultra conservative and she's an avant-garde liberal."

Jesus Solved the *Conflict*

That was 30 years ago. The way I look at it, God put me in a position where I could not run away, which was my pattern. I HAD to stay married this time! He was a person I loved spiritually, a man I respected and a person who was strong and balanced. I knew I had to stay married, I couldn't run away. *My Conflict*, which had destroyed other meaningful relationships, had been mitigated by the healing power of Jesus. I was now stable enough to withstand the turmoil of marriage. And I now had the Bible to teach me what love really is - 1 Corinthians 13.

The Time Went By

I wasn't a perfect wife. There are things I wish I had done. I did my best at the time. I hope he was happy and satisfied with marrying me.

The other day as I sat in my big brown chair
Looking into the sky, I thought of you,
And the Time Went By.

I was happy and content as The Time Went By.
Then dropped out of the blue sky a humming bird
With all of his colors coming and going
And coming again.

I thought of you and the
Land of Colors – My Angel, My Angel
I was happy and The Time Went By.

E.R.G.

Elmer Never Faltered

Elmer considered that he was assigned by God to marry me. He always looked after Barbara, who lived close to us. When we moved, she moved. We were friends and sisters, having lunch, playing bridge, attending Church. Barbara was a partner in the many business ventures Elmer/we pursued.

Elmer and I taught Bible Studies in the Presbyterian Church during most of our marriage. Elmer was scholarly; I, formerly the "avant-garde liberal" was now the ardent Christian. We made a good team. We both loved God, Jesus and His Marvelous Word. We worked our hearts out for and in the Church to produce: Classes, Plays, Skits, Seminars, yes, and that wonderful Potluck!

Adam's Football Games

Elmer-Rusty was a wonderful man. He said, "I always thought God wanted me to have six children." and embraced my three kids with his whole heart. "We're going to all of Adam's football games." and we did. He was calm, kind, focused, honest and determined. I had never "fallen" for a dependable man like Rusty. He wanted to show and give me the world. He modestly told me, "You'll be a millionaire."

"I'm Not Through With You Yet"

Elmer went on some four years ago. I miss him. My heart hurt after he left. My son Dan was in a play with other teachers. They sang a song in which the main verse was, "Lassie, come away." That sweet beckon seemed to me Rusty calling me to join him in Heaven. I went out in the forest to talk it over, "God, am I going to die?" And God answered, "I'm not through with you yet." And I knew then I was going to finish my book *Why Tears? The Mystery of Your Emotions* and *The Voice in the Volkswagen.* I had also promised Rusty I would edit his book *Your America* written for high school students on the history of America.

This Is My Story

So, Dear Reader, this is my story of How He Got Me and after being got, how he blessed me with a dear husband, a father for the children and a grandfather for the grandchildren. Elmer's business abilities and determination still provide for Barbara, their three children, and me.

Still Friends

The phone just rang. It was Tommy Lloy, the man God put in my life when I was 20 years old, the man who was perfect for me. I have apologized to Tommy for being so erratic and throwing his ring on the ground. He forgives me. We are friends and remember the good times we had.

Freddy Goldberg lives about a half an hour from our place here on the desert. Adam had a Thanksgiving Dinner. Fred came. We visited. It was good to see him and once again acknowledge our love for the children and, perhaps, one another.

For Many Years

For many years, I've had a vision of Rusty and me running toward each other with complete joy in Heaven.

Phase Nine
Who Do YOU Think Jesus Is?

Who Do You Think Jesus Is?

After I met Jesus, my life changed. I became a passionate rescuer, telling others of how he called me out of darkness into his marvelous light. I didn't know I was lost until I was found! Amazing Grace! It doesn't take long for me to rummage through a conversation to perceive the speaker's salvation history.

I like the great question, "Who do you think Jesus is?" I love the great question, "Who do you think Jesus is?" Never is it effective without the Holy Spirit. We can't "talk" someone into believing. It does no good to tell the Tale unless you are showered in the halo of the Holy Spirit. It is He that is roping in His Lost. The Holy Spirit, is able to search out the scattered, the lost and rebellious to bring His own into the Fold.

He stands at the door and knocks. Right now, if you ask Him, He will come in and be with you. He will never leave you.

No matter what you go through, He will go through it with you. What a Guy!!

Julie Cried and Cried

It was my blessing and task to lead many people to the Lord: some, I remember and many more I do not. Bless them. One time ~ ~

Often, when an odd number of students was in my class, I participated as a listening partner. Julie cried and cried. After many listening responses, I asked her to wait after class.

"Julie, there is some thing in you that is crying out for Jesus that you perceive is in me. Jesus is right here, knocking at your heart door." Julie nodded, weeping, and met her Lifelong Partner that very day.

Charlene and the "Upper Room" Baptism

"Char, anyone who wants it can have it. What do you want to do?"

" Yes. How do we do that?"

"Okay, we'll praise God and ask Him to fill you with His Holy Spirit."

We thanked God and praised God. When the Time was right, I asked her to just babble. Char babbled and then came a most beautiful Tongue.

What Do We Praise/Thank Him For?

Praise God for His faithfulness, for his holiness, for love, for creation, for beauty, for kindness, for rightness. Thank God for the sky, the plants, the rain, the soil, your life, your mind, your thoughts, your skills, your children, your breath. You get the idea.

Jack

I offered to introduce Jack to the Lord. We were leading a seminar for his business. You would recognize his famous last name. Jack said, "Johana, there are things I love that I just don't want to give up." Poor Jack. That was 40 years ago. I hope time and wisdom have brought Jack into the Kingdom.

Try and Try Again

We were in Church at a Family Play. When the time seemed right, I asked Jeanine if she wanted to receive Jesus. Jeanine looked at me and said, "No." We sang some songs, and went out into the foyer. Jeanine came to me with tears in her eyes, and simply said, "I'm ready now." We said the humble prayer of inviting the Lord to come in.

Gary

Gary was in Santa Cruz, preparing for a move to Canada. I portrayed Jesus to him. He said, "No, thanks." As he was getting ready to leave, he came to me and said these words, "I'm ready now." And Gary took Him up on His Invitation; right there, loaded truck and all in front of Stapleton's Grocery Store on River Street in Santa Cruz.

"I Said That Prayer in AA"

Another person had received the Lord when attending AA. She didn't follow up through learning anything the Bible has to teach. She doesn't personally proclaim Jesus. No Church, no Bible. She probably doesn't know that once Jesus comes into your life, he doesn't bug out or leave you. He guides, helps, restores and stays right in your heart. She greets her old age with a cheerful heart – almost 90 years young.

My Friend's Daughter

My friend's daughter was determined to kill herself. Several times, she cut her wrists and proclaimed to her mother that she did not want to live. My friend asked if I could help. I called Cerise and asked if I could pray with her. She agreed. I prayed with her that Jesus would surround her with His Spirit and fill her and that He would guard her from negative thoughts. Cerise is now a physical therapist and is happily married.

Mercy Trumps Judgment

That's it, folks. We are forgiven the entire load of wrongs. We are to know that God is Love and we are here, given life, for one purpose, to Love and the path to love is to Forgive and Forgive and Forgive. Jesus shows the Way. Jesus is the Way. God's Beautiful Free Gift. What has one to lose?

Captured by His Holy Crook

You saw how very wrong I was, how many lives I wounded, how off the Path I had gone how I had missed the mark – sinned.

And you can see the miracles and efforts He wrought to drag me kicking and screaming into the Fold. If His Holy Crook could capture someone who was eagerly and passionately pursuing a wrong path, any wrongdoer and non-believer can be brought back to Him.

Ellen's Story

Ellen was separated from her husband and having problems. They had been to counseling. Nothing was working. She wept as she told me her story. I listened.

After, I asked, "Well, Ellen, you have been to counseling, tried everything you could think of to reconcile and it hasn't worked, has it?" "No." she said, weeping. "I know someone who can repair your broken relationship. Would you like to invite Jesus to help you?" "Yes."

"Say this after me, 'Jesus, I ask you to come into my life and repair my relationship with my husband, work everything out and make me the person you want me to be.'"

It took some time, but it happened. Little by little, their marriage thrived. The two live happily together. No Bible study, no Church. "I will never leave you nor forsake you."

I think, deep inside, she knows whom to thank.

Sin

Right now, on our news an argument swells about the homosexuals, citing God's warning in the Word. If you read the Book of Leviticus you will find many rules and regulations, such as: revere your mother and father; do not rob your neighbor; do not charge interest on your loans; do not sow your field with two kinds of seed nor wear a garment of cloth made from two kinds of material; do not make cuttings in your flesh or tattoo any marks upon you; do not want that which another has. And on and on with detail after detail of rules by which the early Jews were to live. Tough to be the Chosen People in the Olden Days!

Along Comes King Jesus

Here comes King Jesus bearing forgiveness and love, telling us **Mercy Trumps judgment. Forgiveness Trumps "You're Wrong." Love Trumps Condemnation.**

He tells us whoever keeps the whole Law but breaks one Law or Commandment, just one!! Is guilty of breaking all. Just one little bitty – "Oh, I wish I had one of those like Doreen has." Where does this leave us? We are all guilty. Is the homosexual or the adulterer or the envious or the liar or the wearer of multiple materials more guilty than another? The Word tells us we are all guilty. ALL HAVE SINNED AND FALL SHORT of God's plan for us.

So what does this mean for us, here, now, in the year 2014, in the United States of America? We're sunk!!! We are no better than another. We're all in the same boat, like it or not!

"Nothing Like That Ever Happened to Me"

A few long time Christians have heard my story and disappointedly said,

"Nothing like that ever happened to me."

"You feel cheated."

"Yes, I have had a secure, calm life. Nothing very exciting happened."

"Just think, Carolyn, you have been sheltered in His Arms all your life. You haven't destroyed anyone's life. Your children are shielded."

My precious one
In what breezy land do you fly your little kite?
My heart grieves

The written word kills - The Spirit gives life.

I Have Written for You

These words I have written – for you. These written words are empty. Only when the Spirit breathes Life into your spirit do these words have Life for you.

I Want Him

God bless you and keep you. If you desire to welcome Jesus into your life, this simple prayer will do it. You see, he's waiting, right now, right here for you!

"Jesus, come into my heart.
Be my Lord and Savior
and make me the person
God wants me to be."

And, then, I will say, *"Where is Jesus now?*
And you will say, *"In my heart."*
And I will say, *"He will never leave you nor forsake you."*

Amen and Amen

Why did God go to all of that trouble?

    Smoking
    The Voice in the Volkswagen
    The Bright Light
    My Name is John
    Topaz and the Potluck
    Phillip
    Stripped Bare
    Rusty

Why me?
    I just shake my head with incredulous, deep,
        mindboggling, dazed thankfulness.

LOVE

Jesus was at dinner. A woman of the street entered and began to wash his feet and dried them with her own hair. Simon was disgusted, "Doesn't he know what kind of person she is?"

Jesus, knowing what Simon is thinking says, "A certain businessman is owed money: one person owed $50.00; the other $500.00. When they could not pay, he forgave them both. Which one will be more grateful?"

Simon answers, "I guess the one who was forgiven the most."

And Jesus says, "You have guessed rightly, Simon. Her sins, which are many, are forgiven, for she loved much."

And to the woman of the street, Jesus says,

" Your sins are forgiven.
Your faith has saved you.
Go in peace."

Extra Stuff

A Pile of Gold

A person wandered through life, searching for something, making lots of mistakes.

And then the person came upon a beautiful pile of gold and jewels. It was just sitting there, free for her to have.

She wanted to tell everyone she knew, and loved about the pile of gold and jewels and how having them helped her and her life

And so she did. Some didn't care. And some didn't like hearing about it.

But there were some who went with her
There was so much gold and jewels. There was plenty for all.

And it was free!!

The Light to Change ~

They chatted as they walked down the sidewalk.
Seated in the alcove was a man.
"A drunk", she guessed.
He held out his hand.
Her body stiffened as they passed.
They waited for the light to change.
Something moved her to the side of the man.
She slipped her left hand in her pocket
She held the two quarters out to the man.
Her words seemed strange.
"Sorry to see you so down and out, Brother."
The Man took her hand in a courtly, old-fashioned way
and kissed it.
He looked up at her with eyes that entered her heart.
Eyes that cleared a passage.
Eyes she cannot remember but will never forget.
The Man with the eyes of an Angel said simply,

"My name is John."

Dear Young Person,

The Given

This is the situation: We are all born little babies, pure, innocent and beautiful. Somewhere, sometime, along the way, things happen to us: hurt feelings, wounded hearts, disappointments, feel cheated or left out. And then, negative ideas come to us that seem like solutions to our hurts. Thoughts like: anger; I'll get even; I'm no good; just wait, I'll get you back; they don't love me. If we accept and believe them, they can affect beliefs and decisions that lead us down a wrong and possibly hurtful path that can mess up our lives.

God in Camouflage!

God knew we could not stay pure and innocent and that somewhere along the way, we would believe on the negative. God didn't want to lose us to the negative. Oh woe, what to do.

His solution was to create a perfect person, (actually God Himself disguised as Jesus - God in camouflage!) Jesus was a perfect person. He never gave in to the negative even though He was very tempted - "Ah, come on Jesus. You could rule the world. Have anything you want." He even stayed pure unto being killed by people who hated him.

Jesus Can Clean Up the Mess

So, when or if a person - you - or, I - or anyone believe Jesus will guide, protect and help you, that person can ask Jesus to come into his or her heart and guide, protect and help you.

Once He comes in, he doesn't leave. He says, "I'll never leave you." He sticks with us through thick and thin. Jesus is able through that Spirit to cleanse our hearts and lives from the hurts we have experienced and clean up the mess from any wrong decisions we made.

What If They Never Heard of Jesus?

Now, some people, a lot, have never heard of Jesus. Or, if they have, they don't believe. This might be confusing but the Holy Spirit will tell you what to believe and what not to believe!

Why do some people believe? And some people don't believe? That is a wonderful question.

"My Sheep"

"My sheep hear my voice." What is His Voice? The Holy Spirit. Who are His Sheep? Those who hear His Voice. The Holy Spirit is sometimes called "The Hound of Heaven". What does a hound do? Searches and searches for those who Jesus is calling.

When we ask Jesus to come into our hearts, we are inviting the perfect person: God, Love, Spirit to come into us, to guide us, to protect us and to make us as perfect as we can be. It's just that simple.

Saved From What?

It is called "salvation" ~ being saved. Saved from what? The negative. It is also called "deliverance". Delivered from what? Delivered, from the negative.

Other Folds

Jesus does say, "I have other folds you do not know about." Well, I don't know about them (He was right!) however I know that "folds" means a place where the sheep are and He is the Great Shepherd.

There is a lot of mystery here! That makes it fun!

Knock, Knock

Jesus always says, "I am standing at your door. If you invite me, I will come in and be with you."

Remember Aslan in the Narnia Books? Aslan is Jesus.

"Teacher! Teacher!"
— ANTHONY, PRE-SCHOOL

The teacher expands the personal growth and development of each student and is especially able to enhance the inner potential of every explorer.

Portrait of the Teacher © Prometheus Nemesis Book Company

CPSIA information can be obtained at www.ICGtesting.com
Printed in the USA
BVOW10s1002221114

376261BV00007B/10/P